*R*ocky Mountain National Park affords visitors a glimpse of the abundant wildlife that once defined the character of the West. Symbolizing power, beauty, and the excitement of discovery, the magnificent American elk rewards patient observers in the wildness of our nation's tenth oldest national park. Each fall, the eerie sound of bugling bull elk echoes off valley walls and across open meadows as competition for elk cows heightens.

*L*ate afternoon shadows sweep across the northern flanks of Longs Peak as the last rays of golden light warm Trail Ridge Road. Cloaking Forest Canyon below, the cool veil of evening begins its reign over the land. Darkness stills this tundra world until the morning sun appears.

Front cover: Autumn gold decorates Bear Lake below Hallett Peak, photo by Jeff Gnass. Inside front cover: Brilliant Parry primrose thrive in precious park wetlands, photo by Glenn Randall. Page 1: A powerful bull elk emerges from a stream, photo by Don George. Pages 2/3: From Trail Ridge, Longs Peak is illuminated by an amber sunset, photo by J.C. Leacock. Pages 4/5: The Colorado River reflects springtime in the Kawuneeche Valley, photo by Salvatore Vasapolli.

***Rocky Mountain National Park**, located in north central Colorado, established in 1915, preserves the massive grandeur, rich scenery, wildlife and wildflowers of the Rockies' Front Range.*

Edited by Cheri C. Madison
Book design by K. C. DenDooven

First Printing, 1995
in pictures ROCKY MOUNTAIN The Continuing Story
© 1995 KC PUBLICATIONS, INC.
LC 95-75098. ISBN 0-88714-085-8.

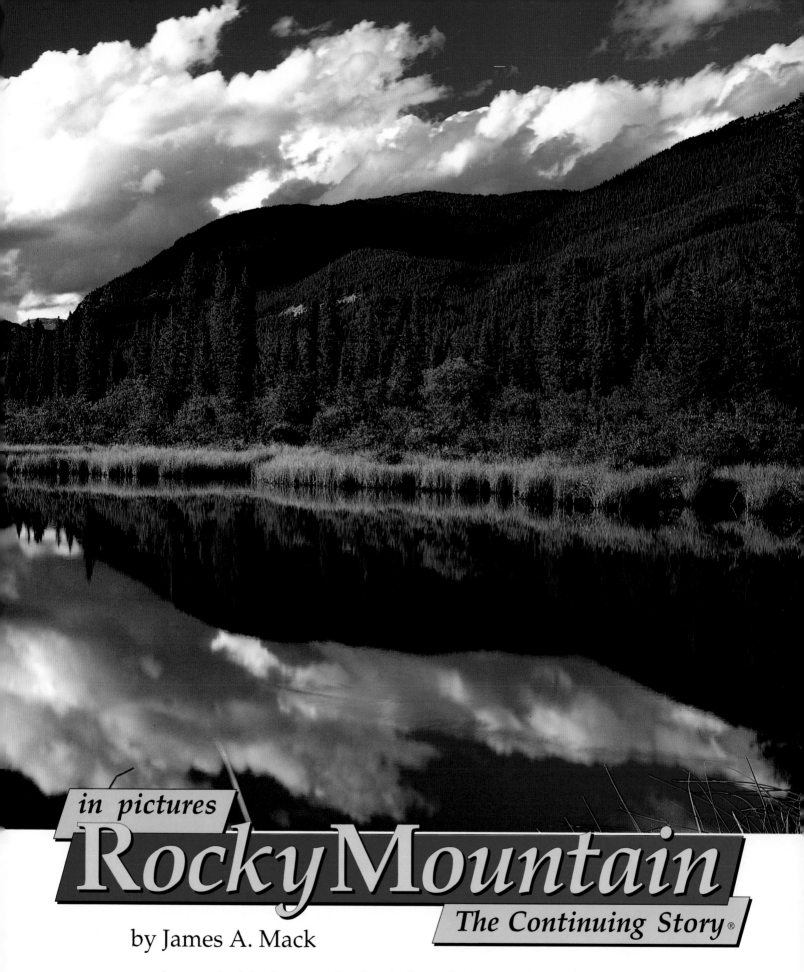

in pictures

Rocky Mountain
The Continuing Story®

by James A. Mack

James A. Mack earned a Bachelor of Science degree in wildlife management from California State University at Humboldt. He has lived and worked in nine park service areas over 26 years. Jim is currently the chief naturalist at Rocky Mountain National Park and has been actively engaged in developing an environmental education program.

National park areas are special landscapes set aside by acts of Congress to protect and preserve features of national significance that are generally categorized as scenic, scientific, historical, and recreational.

As Americans, we are joint caretakers of these unique places, and we gladly share them with visitors from around the world.

Adorned with countless natural gems, Rocky Mountain National Park is one of the crown jewels of our park system. This national treasure continues to rank high on the list of places to visit, not only as a once-in-a-lifetime trip, but as a compelling destination for people to return to generation after generation. Nearly one-third of the park lies above tree limit in what first appears to be an austere environment. Yet this unique landscape is inhabited by numerous specially adapted organisms. Via Trail Ridge Road, millions of visitors can experience this circumpolar ecosystem rarely found south of the Arctic Circle.

Lightly dusted by snow, Rock Cut frames Longs Peak while lingering clouds flood Forest Canyon below.

JIM OSTERBERG

Diversity

From serene mountain meadows to the jagged peaks of the Continental Divide, Rocky Mountain National Park is a setting of diversity. Home to 66 species of mammals and over 900 species of plants, the park and surrounding lands are a treasure chest of life.

The key to the park's diversity lies in its vertical nature. The asphalt ribbon of Trail Ridge Road laces together three distinct plant communities that can be distinguished by the observant visitor. Identifying these ecosystems enables people traveling through the park to determine elevation. Recognizing the ponderosa pine forest on the eastern side of the park places the traveler at 7,800 to 9,000 feet, while the subalpine spruce/fir forest is generally found between 9,000 and 11,400 feet. Alpine tundra blankets the park above 11,400 feet, where tree limit marks the beginning of this unique arctic environment.

Each element of this varied landscape is precious, from the smallest wildflower to the massive moose. Designated as an International Biosphere Reserve in 1976, the national park has set aside special areas for ongoing research. By documenting changes that occur over time, the integrity of these ecosystems may be preserved for the future.

▲ **Carved by ancient glaciers and sculpted by wind and water, the park is a** world of endless dimension. Alpine tundra rolls gently over the landscape, spilling down toward forested slopes that shelter wildlife. Rocky crags etch unforgettable impressions into skies that offer fascinating displays of clouds and color. Minute worlds of lichens and mosses wear away the land at an unimaginably slow pace.

The tenacity ▷ *of life is exemplified by the wind-shaped form of this limber pine. Growing out of rock, its roots cling to the earth, fighting against the powerful forces of harsh winds and mountain weather.*

*R**ecovering from local extinction and** ◭ found with increasing frequency on the west side of the park, the river otter is living proof that humans can succeed at rebalancing nature's equation through restoration efforts.*

◀ *A** magpie scolds a passing coyote** as the two scavengers exchange glances. Coyotes are frequently seen in open meadows where their yips and howls often accent evenings around a campfire.*

Glass Lake is one of the park's 147 clear and cold, sapphire ornaments that are frequent destinations for hikers and backpackers. Reflecting the intense blue sky, these alpine gems are most often nestled at the base of rocky escarpments, where their waters serve to refresh the human spirit.

JAMES FRANK

Fewer people visit ▷ to experience the fresh snow and crisp air of winter. However, snowshoeing is a rapidly increasing way for people to explore the solitude and beauty of the park's backcountry. Having the proper equipment, keeping a watchful eye on the weather, checking avalanche conditions, and talking with park rangers all contribute to making such excursions safe and rewarding.

JAMES FRANK

A Balance Between People and Nature

JOE ARNOLD JR.

▲ **T**he western wood lily is a rare wildflower of moist environments with distinctive red-orange petals and dark maroon anthers. A common sight within the park are the yellow heart-shaped petals of cinquefoil, or potentilla.

JOE ARNOLD JR.

▲ **C**limbers are challenged by the granite walls of Lumpy Ridge. These soft-looking, rounded formations have whimsical names like Twin Owls, the Bookends, Batman Rock, and the Pear.

Considered the ▶ highest continuous paved road in the nation, Trail Ridge Road offers cyclists sweeping vistas of grand scale while providing vignettes of the miniature world of alpine tundra.

JAMES FRANK

Wildlife at the Park

The opportunity to capture a glimpse of wildlife is the reason that four out of five people say they visit Rocky Mountain National Park. Observant visitors are rarely disappointed, since the park offers access to such varied wildlife habitats.

Because of the 4,400-foot gain in elevation along Trail Ridge Road, this highway connects three distinct ecosystems, each with its own communities of plants and animals. A trip along the high mountain route is equivalent to a journey of over 2,400 miles north, bringing the car-bound traveler to worlds more commonly found at the Arctic Circle.

Despite its 415 square miles, the park still does not incorporate a complete ecosystem. As a result, area wildlife depends heavily upon adjacent forest lands and private property for its health. Elk, deer, moose, bighorn sheep, bear, mountain lion, coyote, and fox are among the larger species found within the park. A host of smaller animals like marmots, pikas, ground squirrels, chipmunks, and rabbits add to the array of animal life. There are also over 260 recorded species of birds found in the park, occupying a variety of habitats at every elevation.

As with many of our national parks, the delicate balance of life is upset when elements are missing from the ecosystem. In Rocky Mountain, the wolf and the grizzly have long since been extirpated from the habitat, changing nature's course forever. Recent work to preserve the heritage and diversity of the park has seen many success stories, though. The river otter, the greenback cutthroat trout, and the peregrine falcon are three species that, with our help, have reclaimed their inheritance of the ecosystem and now enrich our lives.

The rewards found in viewing wildlife are proportional to the time, energy, and methods used to enjoy the pursuit. Knowing animal habitat and behavior, as well as wildlife watching etiquette, help to ensure successful viewing. Remaining quiet, viewing from a distance, and respecting their natural behavior reduce stress on wildlife.

WENDY SHATTIL / BOB ROZINSKI

▲ *G*reat winter herds of elk roam for forage as they await the greening of spring vegetation. As the* *progression of new plant growth marches up the mountains, bull elk lead the way to summer grazing areas.* *Smaller groups of elk then separate from the herd for the remainder of the season. This ongoing procession of* *wildlife in the park is reminiscent of the frontier days of the West. Part of our national heritage, this abundant* *resource keeps us rooted to our wilder beginnings, despite the fact that most of our instinctive connections to* *the earth have been lost over time.*

The wapiti, or American elk, is the center of attention for wildlife watchers. Elk are best observed in the early morning and evening as they graze along the meadow edges. Gregarious by nature, the elk have grown accustomed to park visitors when viewed from the roadside, but become nervous when approached on foot. Elk were hunted to extinction in the area now known as Rocky Mountain National Park, but restoration efforts in 1913 and 1914 have provided visitors today with the pleasures of watching these regal animals. In fact, park biologists are concerned about the number of elk; black scars on the trunks of the aspen trees may be indicative of too many elk for the available habitat. As human development encroaches on park boundaries, an insular condition has been created, concentrating elk from adjacent lands to areas within the park.

CONNIE TOOPS

The Keepers of the Land

Mountain ▶ lions are the largest predators in the park. Sightings of this magnificent cat are becoming more frequent, although it is not known if their population is increasing. They hunt mostly at night, and their diet consists mainly of deer or, occasionally, elk.

DON GEORGE

Balancing the needs of wildlife and the desire for visitors to enjoy the pleasures of viewing them is one of the greatest challenges facing park managers today. The sheep crossing zone in Horseshoe Park causes traffic jams and attracts large crowds during the early part of summer. Bighorn sheep are attracted to the natural mineral licks around Sheep Lakes to supplement their diet ▽ before the vegetation matures at higher elevations.

CLAUDE STEELMAN

▲ **An efficient hunter of small prey** such as rabbits, mice, and birds, the bobcat is frequently found in shrubland and along forest edges. This, combined with its nocturnal habits, causes the bobcat to be seen infrequently.

KENT & DONNA DANNEN

▲ **The red fox is most often viewed near** bodies of water, within or near to forest edges. Much more secretive than coyotes, they feed on small rodents, birds, and fruit.

Primary indicators of a riparian ▷ ecosystem's health, amphibians such as salamanders are the subject of ongoing research in the park.

WELDON LEE

◁ **The greenback** cutthroat trout was brought back from the edge of extinction and is now found in several park waters.

ROBERT & JEAN POLLOCK

America's natural wonders have been set aside and protected for all to enjoy.

Our colorful and informative books are a permanent reminder of the beauty in these special areas.

Evidence of beaver activity can be seen at many locations on the east and west sides of the park. The beaver is the largest rodent in North America and actively manipulates the environment to suit its needs. Its construction of dams sets a series of successional events into motion that leads to habitat changes. Siltation, encroaching vegetation, and loss of materials for maintenance of dams and lodges eventually cause the beaver to seek a new home.

Birds

▲ **The gray jay is a common resident of the** park and is found most frequently in the evergreen cover of coniferous forests.

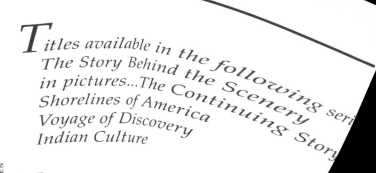

▲ **A year-round resident of the alpine tundra,** the white-tailed ptarmigan is in the mid-stages of changing from its all-white winter plumage to the mottled brown colors of its summer attire.

▲ **Western wood-pewees are challenging to identify** in the field. The best indicator for this member of the flycatcher family is the rapid flipping of its tail.

◀ **Feeding mostly on seeds and insects, the brown-capped** rosy finch nests above timberline. It descends to lower elevations outside the park during the winter months.

ROBERT & JEAN POLLOCK

▲ **V**isitors are more likely to hear the metallic whirring sound of the broad-tailed hummingbird than to see this common resident of the Rockies.

Using its tail as a support, ▶ the northern flicker bores holes into tree trunks searching for insects.

KENT & DONNA DANNEN

GLENN VAN NIMWEGEN

▲ **T**he showy black and gray Clark's nutcracker is frequently seen at overlooks "begging" for food. Visitors can help maintain its wild nature by not feeding it.

The prominent crest ▶ of the Steller's jay gives this common bird a regal look.

The Forest Floor

Distinct forest types reveal themselves as travelers ascend Trail Ridge Road. On the east side, the park-like ponderosa pine forest of the montane ecosystem dominates the landscape to an elevation of about 9,000 feet. Slow, creeping grass fires help maintain the open character of this forest, with the thick bark of the mature ponderosa resisting fire, allowing these patriarchs to live for hundreds of years.

On the western side of the Continental Divide, ponderosa is replaced by its elevational equivalent, the lodgepole pine. Lodgepole are also found in pockets east of the Divide but not in the abundance found in the Kawuneeche Valley. The birth and death of lodgepole forests are frequently linked to fire. While many of the lodgepole cones are destroyed by fire, resin protects the seeds held within some of the cones, and it is only when they are heated that the seeds are released. Within weeks of a fire, new lodgepole seedlings pop up, often competing with post-fire pioneers in the plant world. Individual trees and groves of Douglas-fir and quaking aspen punctuate both the ponderosa and lodgepole forests, depending on local environmental conditions.

The highest major forest ecosystem is the subalpine spruce/fir forest. Colder and much moister conditions prevail at these higher elevations. Dense and abundant forest floor cover makes this forest serve as a moisture reservoir, accumulating snow blown off the tundra and slowly releasing it to streams and creeks all summer long to feed lower elevations. Fire is not a significant factor in sustaining this forest type, but the scars from passing fires may last for decades.

SCOTT T. SMITH

A *blaze of autumn glory punctuates the green of the coniferous* ▲
forest. Cold nights and decreasing sunlight in fall trigger aspen leaves to slowly turn yellow. Groves of aspen trees often develop from the same root system resulting in a uniform changing of color.

The clouds that ▷
blanket Forest Canyon
contribute critical
moisture to the plant
life covering its slopes.
At the bottom of the
canyon, the Big
Thompson River
accepts the moisture
fed to it by unnamed
tributaries as it hurries
to the eastern plains.

SALVATORE VASAPOLLI

KENT & DONNA DANNEN

▲ *Anxious to capture the*
spring sun, the snow buttercup
wages a delicate war on winter.

The lodgepole pine forest along ▷
the trail to Ouzel Falls is rapidly
recovering from a 1978 fire. Releasing
valuable nutrients to the soil and
opening the forest floor to increasing
sunlight, the fire helped the forest
understory spring to life.

JOHN WARD

A Crown of Color

Delicate pink ▷ flowers of moss campion decorate the alpine tundra in early summer. The cushion growth form of this hearty plant protects it from the ravages of winds at high elevations.

▲ **W**estern yellow paintbrush blooms in the park's subalpine and alpine ecosystems throughout summer. Hybrids vary in color from rose to bright purple.

◁ **G**rowing alongside purple asters, the blue columbine, Colorado's state flower, rewards visitors to the park with its showy and elegant appearance.

▼ **T**apered petals of black-eyed Susans appear like golden stars to dot montane meadows throughout the park.

KENT & DONNA DANNEN

JOHN WARD

▲ **G**olden banner competes with Indian paintbrush to produce a colorful summer show. The brilliant red hue of the paintbrush is displayed not by petals, but by bracts that attract pollinators such as hummingbirds.

Pollen released by Englemann spruce ▷ and subalpine fir cones accumulates on the shores of the Loch beneath Andrews Glacier.

JAMES FRANK

SALLIE G. SPRAGUE

▲ **T**he royalty of the stonecrop family, king's ◁ crown and queen's crown sedum, gracefully ornament the park. Dark red blossoms of king's crown are found in late July throughout the alpine tundra. The rose-colored queen's crown occasionally paints streamside environments in all ecosystems.

Overleaf: The austere east face of ▷ Longs Peak is bathed in morning light. Photo by Joe Arnold Jr.

The Forces that Carve Mountains

Wind, water, ice, and changing temperatures continually sculpt the mountains of Rocky Mountain National Park. The cycle of uplift and erosion had been repeated at least three times before it presented the Rocky Mountains of today. Each of these earlier Rocky Mountains were eventually eroded away. About 16 to 21 million years ago, the latest episode of uplift pushed the summits to their present elevations of over 12,000 feet.

Alpine glaciers have been the major force that has given the park its distinctive topography. A gradually cooling climate and increasing rainfall, turning to snow and ice, caused glaciers to form and, under their own weight, begin to move ponderously across the landscape.

Grinding, plucking rock from canyon walls, and reshaping valley floors to broad U-shaped canyons, these ice flows sculpted the mountains. When exploring the geology of the park the erosional features left by these glaciers offer textbook examples of glacial action. Another unusual geologic feature of the park, and one not often associated with the granite peaks of the Rockies, is the evidence of volcanic activity. On the park's east side Lava Cliffs are formed from welded ash flow tuffs that originated from volcanic vents in the northern portion of the Never Summer Mountains. Specimen Mountain and the Crater, west of the Continental Divide, are remnants from the late Eocene and early Oligocene epochs of about 36 million years ago.

◀ **O**verwhelming views greet hikers within short distances of park trailheads. The trail to Lake Haiyaha provides an almost intimidating panorama of Longs Peak and the Keyboard of the Winds.

The sun's warmth ▶ quickly vanishes as winter storms move in over the backbone of the Continental Divide. Wind speeds sometimes reach 170 miles per hour, causing wildlife to retreat to the shelter of the forests below.

▼ **I**ce-age action carved glacial cirques out of granite mountainsides. U-shaped valleys remain where rivers of ice flowed through existing valleys, grinding the steeper sides into the soft shapes of a sculptured landscape.

WELDON LEE

JOHN BARGER

Combining Forces

The myriad ▶
forces of water
continue to shape
these mountains.
Geologic uplift has
provided the
gradient for running
and frozen water to
wear away the
granite of the
Rockies. Melt
waters from Taylor
Glacier flow into
Sky Pond and the
Lake of Glass,
culminating in
Timberline Falls.
Robert Sterling
Yard, a publicist
and early advocate
for national parks,
named the falls.

JIM OSTERBERG

Blasted by hurricane-force winds, skeletons of limber pines lean above the gnarled branches of krummholz clinging to life at treeline.

The jagged rock ▷ spires along Old Fall River Road were above the reach of glacial action. But expansion of freezing water in tiny crevices causes the rocks to crumble, a process known as frost-wedging.

JOHN WARD

JOHN WARD

▲ **L**ake of the Clouds lies at the base of Mount Cirrus in the Never Summer Range. The lake's name is the culmination of a playful series of identifiers of nearby mountain peaks. Named for cloud formations, Mounts Stratus, Nimbus, and Cumulus are all over 12,000 feet in elevation.

Ptarmigan Needles ▷ guards the crystal waters of Lake Nanita at the terminus of the North Inlet Trail. Hikers on the park's west side generally travel farther through open meadows than east side visitors, yet the rewards of spectacular alpine lakes are just as great.

Lakes of All Shapes and Colors

JACK OLSON

KENT & DONNA DANNEN

Black Lake rewards hikers in the ▲
Glacier Gorge area. Its sheer depth and
steep-walled enclosure combine to give the
lake its dark color.

▲ **E**merald Lake
draws its name from
the sunlight playing
in its shallow depths.
The outlet creek
cuts through a
glacial moraine dam
that originally
created the lake.

KENT & DONNA DANNEN

Gem Lake ▶
passively collects
rainwater and
snowmelt. It has
neither an inlet nor
an outlet.

Water Flows

◀ **V**eils of water flow westward from the Continental Divide over Cascade Falls. Countless streams in Rocky Mountain National Park feed the Colorado River and a thirsty West.

MICHAEL LICHTER

Determined ▷ hikers are rewarded by solitude at Lake Husted in the northeastern section of the park. This remote area of the Mummy Range contains a portion of the headwaters of the Big Thompson River which supplies water to the northern Front Range communities of Colorado.

JOHN WARD

▲ **An early autumn snow blankets the shores of Lake Irene and dusts the subalpine firs near** Milner Pass. The first snows present a tranquil scene, but soon the harsh winds will strip the leaves from the plants and rattle the branches. The changing of the seasons provokes increased activity for wildlife as they work to store food, or forage to add weight for the stresses of the winter ahead. Plants, on the other hand, have begun the process of shutting down for the winter.

▲ **Winter's grip holds the tundra of the Mummy Range in its icy grasp as hurricane-force winds blow** snow into a blinding fury. At lower elevations, the forested slopes of Hidden Valley show only a light dusting of snow. Winter weather patterns bring moisture-laden storms from the Pacific, but air is stripped of its humidity as it spills over the Continental Divide, creating a rainshadow on the eastern slope. Winds—both arctic blasts and warming downslope chinooks—are constant weather factors on the eastern side of the Rockies, particularly in the winter. These currents also pull what little moisture remains from vegetation. The icy winds of winter are called "Alberta Clippers" and originate from high in the Canadian Provinces, occasionally keeping the park locked in sub-freezing temperatures for days at a time.

Winter

JOHN WARD

JAMES FRANK

▲ **Shrouds of ice flow over coarse granitic rock near** Black Lake. Like miniature glaciers, ice at this smaller scale exhibits the erosional processes that carved the spectacular canyons and valleys of the park. The most commonly exposed metamorphic rocks are gneiss and schist. Usually quite angular and often forming knife-like ridges and craggy peaks, these formations stand in dramatic contrast to the more rounded granite features scoured by advancing alpine glaciers.

People at the Park

During the spring, fall, and winter, visitors can find the solitude and quietness that they may be seeking. But the summer months typically find the park crowded, at least along the major corridor to Bear Lake and Trail Ridge Road. The park receives over 3 million visitors each year, which is about the same number visiting Yellowstone National Park annually. The difference is that Rocky Mountain National Park is about one-eighth the size of the nation's oldest park.

Rocky Mountain has been a family vacation destination for generations. Parents and grandparents return for the experience they had as children but they are now bringing their own children and grandchildren to recapture the joyful memories of their youthful visit. Many visitors have remarked how unchanged the park has remained despite the increased volume of people. Park managers have taken these observations as the highest compliment for having achieved the dual mandate of the National Park Service: "...to conserve the scenery and the natural and historic objects and the wild life therein, and to provide for the enjoyment of the same in such manner and by such means as will leave them unimpaired for the enjoyment of future generations."

But that achievement has not come without a struggle. To preserve the visitor experience, the park has been forced to resort to a reservation system for campgrounds. High-use areas like the Bear Lake Trail have been paved in recent years to minimize trail damage, along with being fenced to reduce trail expansion and impact to adjacent vegetation. For the most part, people have been willing to accept these measures in exchange for being able to experience the park.

The question remains as to what additional measures may be necessary to continue to preserve not only the parks themselves but the experience that most visitors come to expect and enjoy. Increasing numbers may lead to reservations for simply entering a park, along with daily and overnight limits on the numbers of people.

Fall colors ▶
welcome hikers to
over 350 miles of
trails. National parks
are more than
superlative scenery
and frozen moments
in our national history.
They are places for
personal reflection
and re-creation of our
human spirit.

◀ **A** lone elk
crosses Bear Lake
Road, taking
advantage of the quiet
hours of morning and
the low traffic volume
in early spring.
Named for the "Y"
shape on its face,
Mount Ypsilon
provides a snowy
backdrop.

JAMES FRANK

◀ **C**lear, cool
waters that are the
favorite habitat of
cutthroat, brook,
brown, rainbow, and
greenback trout
beckon anglers to
streams and ponds
throughout the park.
Experienced fly
fishermen enjoy the
challenge of observing
these species and
determining their
behaviors.
Catch-and-release
regulations apply in
many park waters
where native
greenback cutthroat
are recovering from
near extinction.

MICHAEL LICHTER

37

The East Face of ▷ Longs Peak—The Diamond—has served as a training ground for technical climbers working up to the challenge of the world's greatest mountains including Mt. Everest. Non-technical routes to the summit of Longs exist, but climbers must plan their trip carefully and start early in the day to be off the summit before afternoon thunderstorms.

JAMES FRANK

Opening Trail ▷ Ridge Road each spring challenges the best of equipment and operators. Drifts of 25 feet and more are encountered, and crews must fight late spring snowstorms to open the road by Memorial Day weekend.

JOE ARNOLD JR.

The first recorded ascent of the East Face of Longs Peak was in September of 1922. The immensity and scale of this sheer rock face can only be appreciated by finding the five tiny human figures in both pictures (look for a red shirt).

ED COOPER

ED COOPER

JOHN WARD

▲ **H**ayden Gorge is seen in the distance
from the Ute Trail. This trail crosses Trail Ridge
Road just below Forest Canyon Overlook and
provides the hiker with expansive views to the
west and an exciting opportunity to explore the
alpine tundra environment.

WENDY SHATTIL / BOB ROZINSKI

▲ **T**he tiny pika, known by a variety of
names, is a denizen of the alpine tundra. This
active relative of the rabbit is especially
hardworking in the summer months, storing
vegetation in small hay piles to help it survive
the winter months.

JACK OLSON

▲ **M**aking a late summer appearance, the arctic
gentian is a circumpolar species botanically linking the
tundra ecosystems found in Siberia as well as in the
higher latitudes of North America.

Alpine sunflower ▶
and whiproot clover
contribute to the artist's
palette against the rocky
crags of the skyline. The
large alpine sunflower
always faces east,
meeting the first sunlight
of the day.

▲ **Park ranger-naturalists treat**
visitors to an in-depth exploration of
the plant communities and
adaptations for survival in a world
where the growing season may last
only six weeks!

Evidence of prehistoric ▶
people using the park is scattered,
but some remains like this hunting
blind are found. Prehistoric use of
the area was mostly by hunting
parties following game and
ripening vegetation.

▲ *The character of the West is reflected in the wide open spaces and the opportunity to see the country from the back of a horse. This string of riders passes through the Moraine Park area on the way to an afternoon of both relaxation and adventure.*

Seeing Rocky Mountain

▲ *Climbers approach the Keyhole on Longs Peak. After crossing through this portal the route is marked by red and yellow bullseyes painted on the rocks. The climb proceeds through the Trough, to the Narrows, and finally to the Homestretch. Over 15,000 people a year attempt to reach the summit, but only two-thirds are able to complete the arduous ascent.*

▲ *As if driving out of the past, an appropriately dressed couple round a curve along Trail Ridge Road. The road was constructed with the environment, humans, and machines in mind. Engineers were careful to minimize impact on the tundra and keep grades to less than six percent.*

Park founding father and naturalist ▲ Enos Mills would be proud of the ▶ tradition carried on by the ranger-naturalist staff today. Each summer, the park offers a broad cross section of ranger-led hikes, talks, and evening campfire programs to help the public understand and appreciate the park's resources. Topics include bighorn sheep biology in Horseshoe Park as well as an up-close and personal look at the plants and insects of the area.

◀ **T**he Rocky Mountain Nature Association offers a photographic workshop and a wide variety of other topics for individuals interested in half-day, all-day, and week-long seminars. The non-profit organization is one of the oldest in the national parks and continues to provide substantial support for visitor programs.

Rocky Mountain Nature Association

The Rocky Mountain Nature Association (RMNA) was created to support the educational, scientific, and resource management programs of Rocky Mountain National Park. Over the years, its assistance has been extended to other areas administered by the National Park Service, the U.S. Forest Service, Colorado State Parks, and the U.S. Fish and Wildlife Service.

The Rocky Mountain Nature Association is one of over 60 cooperating associations involved with the national park system nationwide. Established in 1931, RMNA is one of the oldest associations in the nation. Profits generated from the sale of educational materials provide financial support to programs such as the Junior Ranger, park volunteer, and artist-in-residence programs. Citizens interested in providing support to the park are encouraged to join the association to take advantage of its quarterly newsletter on park activities, seminar programs, and discounts on publications.

JOHN BARGER

▲ *The Colorado River in Kawuneeche Valley. It is hard to imagine that the small rivulets of water here eventually contribute to the forces that have carved the Grand Canyon. Equally hard to imagine are the great influences parks may have on the hearts and minds of people of all ages. A visit to Rocky Mountain refreshes the spirit and may contribute to the strength of an individual or a nation.*

SUGGESTED READING

ARMSTRONG, DAVID M. *Rocky Mountain Mammals.* Boulder, Colorado: Colorado Associated University Press, 1987.

BUCHOLTZ, C.W. *Rocky Mountain National Park: A History.* Boulder, Colorado: Colorado Associated University Press, 1983.

CRONIC, HALKA. *Time, Rocks, and the Rockies.* Missoula, Montana: Mountain Press Publishing Company, 1984.

NELSON, RUTH ASHTON. *Handbook of Rocky Mountain Plants.* Estes Park, Colorado: Skyland Publishers, 1979.

SMITHSON, MICHAEL T. *Rocky Mountain: The Story Behind the Scenery.* Las Vegas, Nevada: KC Publications, Inc., 1986.

ROCKY MOUNTAIN NATIONAL PARK

National parks have been called barometers of the nation's environmental health, and for good reason. Until now they have stood, for the most part, at some distance from those influences that have diminished the quality of health in more urban areas. Loss of air quality, congestion, invasion by exotic plants and animals, growth adjacent to park boundaries, light pollution, and other threats are all contributing to a gradual loss of integrity for parks. But the human spirit has been a profound force throughout the course of history and that spirit can see to it that our parks are protected. You are encouraged to contact your nearest or favorite national park or conservation group and offer to contribute to the future.

JOHN WARD

Hallett Peak soars to the sky just above the Bear Lake area as the crisp air of autumn flames the aspen trees into fall colors.

JOHN WARD

▲ **T**here is no question why this body of water in the Mummy Range in the extreme northern part of the park is called Mirror Lake. Seekers of solitude are well rewarded by a hike into this remote area.

Inside back cover: Wintry blasts of ▶ air shape the trees and the drama of the high country. Photo by John Ward.

Back cover: Bighorn sheep guard ▶ the flat summit of Longs Peak. Photo by Kent and Donna Dannen.

Books in this "in pictures ... The Continuing Story" series are: Arches & Canyonlands, Bryce Canyon, Death Valley, Everglades, Glacier, Glen Canyon-Lake Powell, Grand Canyon, Grand Teton, Hawai`i Volcanoes, Mount·Rainier, Mount St. Helens, Olympic, Petrified Forest, Rocky Mountain, Sequoia & Kings Canyon, Yellowstone, Yosemite, Zion.

Translation Packages are also available. Each title can be ordered with a booklet in German, or French, or Japanese bound into the center of the English book. Selected titles in this series as well as other KC Publications' books are available in up to five additional languages.

The original national park series, "The Story Behind the Scenery," covers over 75 parks and related areas. A series on Indian culture is also available. To receive our catalog listing over 90 titles:
Call (800-626-9673), fax (702-433-3420), or write to the address below.

Published by KC Publications, 3245 E. Patrick Ln., Suite A, Las Vegas, NV 89120.

Created, Designed and Published in the U.S.A.
Printed by Dong-A Printing and Publishing, Seoul, Korea
Color Separations by Kedia/Kwangyangsa Co., Ltd.